Holy Week

Holy Week

Poems

Michael Hugh Lythgoe

Foreward by D. Audell Shelburne

To order additional copies of this book, contact:
Xlibris Corporation
1-888-795-4274
www.Xlibris.com
Orders@Xlibris.com
36656

CONTENTS

III THE LATE FORGETTER

Dedicated to my wife, Louise,

and to Liam Rector (*in memoriam* 1949-2007)

When I first met Michael Lythgoe at the annual Writers' Festival at the University of Mary Hardin-Baylor, I had no idea he was a retired Lt. Col. (USAF) who had seen war first-hand in Vietnam. I did not connect this quiet, unassuming gentleman with the poet whose work I had seen in early volumes of *Windhover.* At the time, I couldn't have imagined the depth of this man who finds words to the inner songs of being human in these complicated days. If you have ever heard Mike read, you can't help but hear the passion lurking beneath the controlled delivery. He lets the words do the work, restraining the desire to shout in joy or outrage, to underscore how powerful faith must be to stand firm in empty times.

From the moment we take wing in "Flight Time," the landscape seems foreign, alien. On one level, the poetry of Michael Lythgoe makes everything foreign. His travels through life have taken him far, and the geography of his poems is correspondingly exotic. If you throw in with this guide, you will cross the Ganges, the Rio Tajo, the Tigress, and the Rappahanock River. You will find yourself in the company of Bedouins, Ukukus, and Thai klangs. If you are a typical twenty-first century teenager, you will need an atlas or globe beside you as you read to help you locate Kazakhstan, Slepnyovo, Cuzco, and Cueta. But, no matter how foreign or exotic, the landscapes yield to Mike's artistry, as his brushstrokes draw forth the familiar spirit in place after place.

Lythgoe brings the foreign and familiar together, creates a rich tapestry of life and lives, and he always brings you home. It is something to discover one's home through the eyes of a poet, himself seeing the image through the eyes of an artist, only to find that you had never really seen your home at all. I did exactly that in "Georgia O'Keeffe Remembers Texas." There I see Amarillo, its "wonderful emptiness" and "separation of space with something / beautiful" with "sky blue at the end of the world." I grew up loving the horizon there, never conscious of the "Comanche moons" or (I hate to admit) O'Keeffe's connection to my world. Finding my way home via Lythgoe, I first feel disoriented and then recognize what I love as more familiar and more meaningful as it is filtered through the double lens of O'Keefe and Lythgoe.

Mike devotes much of this collection to ekphrastic poetry, and the interplay of artistic visions, the poet's and the painter's, enriches both traditions. Just as his poetry crosses the globe geographically, it touches a variety of artists and artistic styles, from Monet, El Greco, Degas, Van Gogh, Modigliani, Milton Avery, Bonnard, Philip Morsberger, Frederick Hart, and Andrew Wyeth. Some strokes are simple, like Milton Avery's "wife, Sally, posing nude, with a yellow guitar." Which is accurate and evocative, a concise description of an efficient and minimal painting, "a Wallace Stevens poem, pieces of a lyric in colors." Other poems are perhaps more subtle, such as "Triptych: Manassas Studio," in which the three panels and artists create an aesthetic Genesis as the "trio fulfills the emptiness." All of the ekphrastic poems recommend their subjects to the reader, tantalizing, begging for one to Google the images and to appreciate both the painting or sculpture and the poem.

In the midst of the foreign and familiar, Mike's poems ultimately beckon us home because they deal squarely with life. Pain is part of life. Loss is real and painful. But, Lythgoe assures us in his lines and his delivery, pain and loss are also gifts. "Our task," he tells us in "Black Snake in Cherry Tree," "is to live among the dying." In "Lost Along Harmony Way," "the living lie down with the dead," discovering that though this world is "no utopia . . . we embrace the dirt." Yet, these grave realities are only part of the story in Lythgoe's poetry, which resonates with "the gift of discovering the right way / Grace" and the transformation of heartache into a "gift—an oasis within a holy land." Ultimately, Lythgoe's poetry resonates with the understanding that "love is a longing for our own redemption."

Re-reading that last paragraph irks me because Lythgoe's poetry is no kindergarten Sunday school lesson. My description is too reductive, too pat. His poetry is more dynamic, more complex, more challenging, more ambiguous, and certainly more rewarding. Still, in his poems, wounds are fresh. Scars are real. Sacrifice is holy. Redemption is possible. Love reigns supreme.

There is a Renaissance concept in poetry known as copiousness, a fullness and richness that comes when a poem is complete, expansive, whole. It gains in richness from the texture of the details. It adds depth through the insight and thought of a considerate, kind, and intelligent poet. Michael Lythgoe's work is copious.

D. Audell Shelburne, Editor of *Windhover,*
Belton, Texas
September 3, 2007

Yet, Lord, instruct us so to die
That all these dyings may be life in death.

—George Herbert,
"Mortification"

"Crux Gloria" by Tomas Fernandez

WINGS

Flight Time

Dulles departure: lift-off at sunrise.
The ascension into heaven is on time.
A smear of pinks and golds on the port side.

The pilot says Monticello is below.
For a moment we are lost as time flies.
The earth under clouds turns, eternal, slow.

In Dallas, travelers talk of keeping
Time, exit viewing a pocket watch.
One holds an heirloom from his grandfather.
Seeing the pocket watch, another remembers

His father who stared time in the face.
We walk away from a happy landing.
A stewardess sends us to final destinations:
A stop-watch-world, lives with reservations.

Riding In Kazakhstan

The shepherds ask: *what are you looking for?*
They had flown from Istanbul to Bishkek,
Mounted and rode up—out toward China.

The son of a shepherd was their guide;
Alisher gave them fermented mare's milk.
Herdsmen asked: *What are they looking for?*

No one climbs into thin air for nothing.
Is it gold, is it wives, or horses?
No one journeys to the Tian Shan Mountains

Just to travel high summer meadows.
There is one rule: Never let your riding
Crop slip off your wrist. Lost whip—bad luck.

They ate dried apricots to combat
High altitude sickness in a downpour
Of shooting stars, then slept in a yurt.

Alisher showed them how the round felt tent
Packs easily for the nomadic life. What one
Can take down, many must work to put up.

Alisher the guide gave sweets to the children
In the camp—with their wind-burned cheeks;
He changed—in meditation—into a rock,

Into part of the landscape along
The ancient Silk Road of merchants.
Be like a cloud, or a tree, the guide said,

Learn to see more of the world.
What are they looking for?—This writer who dropped

His riding crop on a steep slope,
Lost in pine needles, and the artist—
Wishing he had more pencil lead

For sketching what it was
They were looking for.

Ivory Bill's Rondeau

The secret is out in the Arkansas swamp.
The woodpecker's face, now on a stamp,
Is Ivory Bill (red head) back from the dead.
Hunters heard what the owls said.
Ghostly grail-bird raps in the swamp.

Mallard ducks told hunters in the tupelo
& cypress maze where the red crest goes—
With white on black wings' trailing edges:
The secret is out.

Even water moccasins in the muck know.
Hovering hummingbirds, revved on reds, show
The crows, who control the woods' leading edge.
Crows keep no secrets, no matter their pledge.
But the Audubon Society was the last to know
Of secret flights in the Arkansas swamp.

Brass Reflections

When sometimes lofty towers I see down-razed
And brass eternal slave to mortal rage

Sonnet LXIV, William Shakespeare

Wars teach warriors to atone for art—cold bronze
Sculpture old as imperial Rome's spit & polish.
Spanish Armada, a half-moon formation, eclipsed.
Top brass-generals—polish their rank but lead
The rank & file in sandy camouflage to storied
Immortality wearing black bars & stars to war;
Dull cloth does not shine in the sniper's eye—
    Like a brass tack—
Nor sparkle as a mirror from desert floor.

The soldier's stuff is flesh & blood, not brass
Knuckles. Men are weaker than metals—with flak
& tracers flying—vests plateless to repel all shrapnel
From flesh & bone. Thick & thin all bleed the same.

Invaders historically deface the saints—holy statuary—
Steal the art of the conquered, rape the treasury.
Often, in the name of religion, warriors make martyrs
Of the faithful, lop off angels' wings, burn
Books & wooden icons, liberate calligraphy,
Enemy gods, leave spent brass in ruined temples.

Long Key

Orion travels over sea-rattles
Of the January night.
The Hunter is a myth over Miami—
Slain for a love he craved in starry space.
He patrols planets above the spray-wet jetty
Near where we lie like driftwood
Burls entwined on sandy shore
In sight of flashing buoy
Blinking survival codes
To astronomers navigating in the keys.
Banished Orion's shadow crosses Havana's
Searching floodlights spotting afterburners'
Flames, as gunboats prowl revolutionary reefs.
The hunter faces fierce snorts
In *the bull ring of the moon,*
Poised to pierce in over the horns
To the stellar heart of Taurus.

Orion, exiled to the galaxies,
Doomed by Diana's jealousy, lights up
The Florida Straits, shines
Above the fighter pilot's sparks
Scarring the lunar face with their flights,
Stirring the sweet, black, *cafecito*-night.

There are scraping sounds
Of keels aground on coral;
Spanish sobs are washing
In from beyond the breakers.
Cubans are slapping down
Their dominoes—white dots in ebony—
On *Calle Ocho.* Orion roams above
Our archipelago seeking cutlass-cut
Cane squeezed into rum, to taste;
He sips the sea-breeze of the keys,
Feeling the uncertain freedoms
Of a wretched refugee.

The Gargoyle's Stare

Remember the gargoyle.
                    —Malcolm Muggeridge

The gargoyle stares as blank as stone,
        Unable to read these lines.
His bloated tongue protrudes;
        He drools like a gutter spout
        On a Gothic cathedral—
Something you'd see on York Minster
        Instead of at the bingo table.
Ever since the medicine prescribed
        For him, perhaps in error,
His gargoyle's face dripped
        Like a bib until . . .
Last night when Death dammed
        Up the perpetual flow.

He was under the care provider's wings,
In the emergency nurse's hands.
She was the one who first heard
        The Gargoyle's muffled heart
Going off as she pumped & pushed
Giving the Kiss of Life through
The slobber & the gag of his gape.
        The surprise? The blast
Of a final heartbeat in his chest.

Now his blind daughter rocks
Retarded, left alone, a resident
In the Nursing Home, leaning like a shop
Along the cobbled street—The Shambles—
Preserved within York's medieval walls.
She calls for her Poppa but hears
Only the stunning interval,
The silent crescendo in her ears.
She cannot comprehend the prayers
Believers mumble under a gargoyle-
Guarded roof somewhere in waxen light
Below the dark cathedral's towers,
The medieval, stony stares.

Wings

A silhouette—
Stick figure blends
Into shadows
Dripping from a willow—
Stalks prey on stilts
In skinny stealth.

A gawky heron
Leans into a step,
Tiptoes through shallows,
Stops . . . and strikes,
Bites, long bill clasps
Fish—a flash and white
Wiggle
Before the swallow.

Turquoise feathers
Fan out, rise off the water
Slowly flap hang
Over the lake—winging
In a mirror below;
Double-heron glides
Settles on the far shore.

Gulls on reconnaissance
     Sweep their targets;
Two sorties recover at home
Base on the Chesapeake.

     Mostly it is still
As a landscape in oils;
On the high side of rain—
In the heavens—an airplane.

I hear the mock of a crow, a crow
Leaving the scene of the incident.

     A sighting:
Great blue heron's ascension.

After A Reading At The Folger Shakespeare Library

(for Charles Wright)

The poet reads Chinese poetry,
Is the scribe of dwarf orchard trees.
He says he dreams eternally of eternity.
His starlight-voice voyages . . . .

Leaving the Elizabethan theater, listeners
Launch on long, free lines into the universe
Of utterance probed by the poet from Tennessee
Who says he no longer believes.

Yet he paints the imagery
Of faithful cathedrals,
Finds it hard to enunciate
His heart-sounds without hymn-sounds,
The vocabulary of his high-church youth.

He fingers his words carefully
As beads, but he prays no rosaries;
He intones other decades,
Religious-sounding litanies,
Memories of Dante's landscape
From when he wore a uniform, a veteran
Teaching Italians American sounds.

The reading ends. He exits stage left.
So it is for all; no curtain call.
The night is black as wet ink brushed
On rice paper. No moon at all—
A downpour soaks listeners to the skin.

Sheltering a soul as it orbits
Is wet work to be in.

Gods On Thin Ice

The bear-men in their woolen masks
Carry no more blocks of glacial ice
On their fur-wrapped backs; Ukukus
Trek the moonlight into thin air.

The gods are melting in Peru;
Ukukus cut no glaciers any more.
The sacred glacier is disappearing.
Still, Ukukus climb in fur cloaks &

Woolen masks in pilgrimage
To *El Senor de Qoyllur Rit'i.*
The glacier ice is healing ice
16,000 feet high in the Andes.

The Quechua gods are melting.
The bear-men cut no more ice
To share with family & livestock;
Ukukus no longer haul icy blocks

Down from the receding glacier
To the valley below Cuzco.
Locals still worship snow-capped
Mountains, gods they call *apus.*

Bear-men end ice-cutting rituals
To save the sacred glacier ice—
Rare tropical sparkles in patches.
Catholic & Quechuan gods in meltdown.

Pilgrims scale the Andes near Cuzco.
Local rituals: scratch for potatoes, weave
Alpaca wool, pray to gods on thin ice.

Black Snake In Cherry Tree

The season receives new words like new seeds,
As the serpent emerges from a hollow tree.
This is the season for ploughs and planting;
Take time to atone for an apple's misdeeds.

The Saharan season floods—a washout—
Unpredictable is spring's renewal;
The winter's discontent is breaking camp.
Immigrant clouds clash along thunder's borders.

We believe in April's Sepulcher, lost
Paradise, fertile air, heavy oak pollen.
Blue grass is fresh; Kentucky foals frolic.
New nests give wing to feathered songs.

A Midas-touched shrub ignites the margins.
Patio is awash with cherry rain.
Cherry tree muscles dogwood—shedding
Pinks like a snake losing its old skin.

Cinco de Mayo lilac's scent is free,
Celebrating Our Lady's sky of blues,
Treading on the serpent tempting Eve.
Yet, a black snake suns in the cherry tree.

Forbidden fruit is the taste of the day;
Banished from a garden, we are like weeds,
So we leave remembering Lucifer—
Languourous in the shade—winning the day.

The tattered remnants stain; fallen blossoms
Are angels' wings, fallen, grounded,
Wind-blown; heat-lightning flash—a burn.
Cancer cells spread like crazy weeds; lessons

To learn of hot flashes and earthy speeds.
Our bodies burn with nuclear wild fires.
This season holds the burning in the bones.
Radioactive seeds will kill the weeds.

But once we have fallen in our garden,
Our task is to live among the dying.
Azaleas lose their colors; the fallen
Angels are the tainted leaves of Eden.

As the seasons move the body decays.
The fruit in the orchard ripens and falls.
Autumn browns, dooms the goldenrods.
A split trunk parts, reaching for the sun,

Stretches a cherry limb from wounded bole;
The rough bark on aging cherry tree
Feels the coils slide out of the hollow dark.
Serpent goes out on a limb to stalk a soul.

Vulture Of The Ganges

She loved the smell of smoke, ashes on the water.
She heard the raucous Hindi music—
When the white-shrouded bodies, draped in marigolds,
Descended the ghat steps, were piled on wood pyres
A meter high, splashed with golden ghee,
Set on fire and floated down the holy river.
Around the bend she waited. Death is a business.

For her Untouchable caste, she preyed, picked gold teeth
From the blackened skulls to sell—the profit in recycled death.
By age thirteen the scavenger of the Ganges lay diseased
Near a dead cow, coughing, infected with gangrene, filth.
A Macedonian nun saved her from the dung with love. Healed,
She vowed before the Cross to work for life, to nurse the sick.
The resurrected one turned from death afloat on burning sticks.

The Narc's Wife Blows Smoke

The automatic fell to the floor
At my feet in the back seat.
The gunmetal gave me a chill
Seeing him tuck it between belt &
Bare belly. A Narc driving
To L'Enfant Plaza; we commuters
Following tail lights burning—
Cigarettes aglow from slow drags.

He did his duty for DEA:
Interdicted "The Golden Triangle,"
Traffickers along Thai klangs,
Hit Bankok's dragons, smack.
The Narc scored street busts,
Corralled the great white horse
Riding from Bogota in NYC veins.

He retired from stakeouts for the Feds,
Lives in a forest, works as a shamus—
Computer forensics, security stuff.
His wife is a smoker from Black & White
Films. They keep geese, guinea hens,
Cats, & a cock with sharp spurs.

Tell me about the snakes.

She flicked her bic, pulled on a filter-tip,
Spoke of the slough where a skeletal oak
Stood, leafless, black, soaking roots.
They heard a series of splashes, she
Said—exhaling—near the deepest swamp.
The tree there was writhing, flinging
Sunning serpents—uncoiling, diving
Moccasins swimming from footfalls.

I still think of it: an infinite rain of snakes
Falling on marshlands! Camel light
Smoke climbing like python vines.

Happy in his work; he locks & loads
His disks & hard drives chasing perps
Online: hackers, haters, pedophiles.
His wife's tales crawl through screens,
Smoke turning like vipers into stories.

Talkman

Above the rivers Tigris
And Euphrates in an A-10 warplane,
On a tank-killing mission at night,
A surface-to-air missile stops
My flight.

I hang in silk
Between hostile fire and heaven,
Hit the Mesopotamian sands,
Land among nomads—
A prisoner in a tribesman's tent.

One of the shepherds
Teases his blade across
My throat; I'm his enemy
Descended from the firmament
Bomb-like. The goat
Is staked to be bled
By Bedouins.

As a POW I meet
Modern men in green tailored
Uniforms, urban brothers
Of the Bedouins who caressed me
With their knives.
I face an ancient fate:
Interrogation. Electrical
Jolts teach treason.

I am wired, plugged-in
Like a commuter to his walkman
On the uncivil streets of D. C.
The jackhammer-tremors
Rattle out my fillings.
I am charged with sins
Of my countrmen, my wing man.

I give my name
    Between bolts and static.
I give my rank
    After lightning strikes.
I give my service number
    In a stammer.

In the cradle of civilization
I rock late in the millennium;

Technology transfers—
A warrior among warriors,
    Looking for honor . . . .

My hosts return
With what I call:
    TALKMAN.

I dread to hear
The human sounds
    TALKMAN
Makes me speak—
Crying out to remain speechless—

A warrior among warriors aching
For honor in a Biblical place,
Where oil wells light
    The arid wastes.

Closing Wounds

I heard Lorca's guitar: five plucked strings,
Each catgut string an open wound, a summer
Of wounds: a knee opened, belly sliced, bullet hole,

A bag draining . . . A botanist once found a plant
In the Congaree Swamp known by native healers
To draw infections out. I see the soldier who lost

Parts of both her legs; she skis in Colorado
For therapy & rehabilitation. Fictional Brother
Cadfael, a monk who once fought as a Crusader,

Learned from the Moors to heal wounds;
A lesson from an enemy in the Holy Land.
The novelist met the medievalist on the page

Of an illuminated manuscript inscribed in a monastery.
But I cannot meet, nor face, the vet with mangled hand
Who begs the surgeon to leave him a finger or two

Please . . . to dress myself. I suppose Walt Whitman
Learned a thing or two of medicine, nursing amputees,
Bathing rotting flesh, in war. The Word made flesh

For five wounds—lanced, nailed—in a spring between
Two thieves. Loss, wounds, absence. A circle of clam
Or oyster shells is a mystery, but the mound of calcium

Left by an ancient people let deciduous trees grow
Where none had grown before—on a barrier island.
Medicine man, shaman, boiled bark & sedge, stopped

The bleeding; packed with moss & prayer the saber slash;
He sutured the wound with sinew pulled through split skin
On a bone needle—like snail shells first pierced, threaded,

Painted by an African artisan dreaming a human body & soul
Whole before early Iberians colored cave walls & sang
To the gods, believing absence an open wound, a hole in the soul.

Smuggling With The Dead

Swimmers are at the mercy of the gods
Between Ceuta & Morocco; some
Smuggle booty; some pay with their lives.

One swimmer is a smuggler who tows
Crates of whiskey & fridges along the coast;
He is one of the *porteadores*.

The smugglers are swimmers who tow
Tires along the coast back to Morocco.
Swim dangers, pay no customs duty.

Tarek is a swimmer who crosses the barrier,
Smuggles four times a day, swims 100 yards
Through the gauntlet of Guardia Civil.

A miserable tide washes in corpses—
Human misery afloat, African hopes
Drowned crossing the Straits of Gibralter.

Swimmers elude the razor wire fences
Keeping illegals from landing in Spain.
Tarek is allowed to swim his smuggled

Goods along the coast by the police
Who do not want the living to land.
Tarek helps police the beach, a lifeguard

For the drowned; he swims to tow the dead,
A smuggler who swims his booty & pays;
He pays a priceless customs duty to smuggle;

With bodies he bribes police, he swims
The corpses found floating in the straits—
To keep dead illegals off Ceutas's beaches.

The Guardia Civil let him smuggle
Booty the other way—to Morocco—
Smuggles away from the Europeans'

Soil. Spaniards see the smugglers go—
Let them swim to Morocco, let Tarek
Swim booty out, bringing only bodies back.

A Stone Map

Some borders are like stone walls,
Others porous as the Rio Grande,
Or fluid as the coast where Morocco
Meets Ceuta; there swimmers smuggle
Goods & daily drown.

Along the Rio Orinoco, I met
The Venezuelan Army captain
In charge of the border outpost;
We joined his troops in the mess hall,
        Ate a stew of mystery meat
        & jungle roots; I held an
Anaconda for pictures. The Captain,
Uncomfortable in English, offered
A toast to friendships among
Officers. Privately, we handled
Our words like unfamiliar gear.

I received a memento: Venezuela—
    A map carved in stone—
Disputed boundary marked—Essequibo
Region, where Venezuelans patrol.
Jagged spear tip mounted on the map
To represent the Gran Sabana mountains,
Flecked with pyrite; fools gold. Farewells.
    In gratitude, I set a Civil war
Book of pictures, battle-maps of Manassas.
The economy later smoked out a president.
    The new leader wears a red beret,
Befriends Fidel. Workers tighten oil spigots.
But border with Guyana-Brazil—Essequibo—
Remains peaceful Solid as the stone map.

The lost orphan of the Holy Land & Balkans—
Peace—struggles with a "road map." Opponents
Steal geography. African diamonds bleed. Wars
Chop limbs, bury mines, rub out lines in Darfur—
Between Sudan & Chad the desert landscape
Seeks vengeance; rebels cross disputed frontiers,
Redraw maps, carve ethnic & religious lines
In sand, ravage refugees. Maps seldom rest in stone.
    Cartography cuts to the bone.

Aviatrix

Looking up is looking back at lift-0ff—borne aloft on rockets,
Boosted missile-like; a navigator exploring out of our world,
Monitoring the burns, the shuttle engines' turns, the thrust—
Guiding a starship—O—through heaven, practicing a rendezvous
With MIR space station; island of Russians, one lone American.

Looking down is looking back on commissioning ceremony,
Pinned with gold bars in the Syracuse U. Chapel, survival training,
Flying through triple-A from Russian guns manned by Cubans
On Grenada. Looking down is looking back on a Caribbean Sea,
A rescue and airlift form a blue-green-lemon and nutmeg island.

Speaking from space, you miss the planetary-pull of home,
Your husband-pilot—a Falcon coach—watching on earth
With your daughter. She flew in your womb before birth—
In the Shuttle Discovery—alien sonogram, floating capsule—
Like Russian dolls, one cup within another O within another.

You were the astronaut with two heartbeats, daughter the echo,
The double beat, the rhythms within you sounding
Off-beat to monitors on the ground in Houston. The moon—O—
Is always female, *La Luna*; you dreamed into a comet's tale
As a woman, steered a shooting star across *La Luna's* face.

Descending like a meteor to a world of tremors, you skim
A touch-down at Cape Canaveral east of Alligator Alley, making
A little history, smiling through your fish bowl, suited for space
Travel, addressing the Press Club, parades—having viewed
     continental
Drifts and desert shifts and ocean tones aglow on satellite photos.

Mother among astronauts—you will keep the other Os
On a long umbilical cord from Mission Control—tethered
Linking space walks to telescopes imaging black holes
Cloud-free of gravity, orbiting in space over hurricane-trackers,
Seas, stormy-eyes, estuaries and shrinking Amazon greens.

Colonel, wearing silver eagles now on your dress blues.
Looking up is looking back at the sun, the O of the moon,
As your daughter looks up, as your husband reads galaxies;
A wife's winking fire rides a flight plan in constellations
Light years away; blinking, long dead stars still arriving.

In Texas, looking back, you remember looking down
In your down-to-earthness, imagining your family grounded,
Homesick for one blue planet—O—full circle within a universe.

(for Colonel Eileen Collins, USAF, Retired)

Leaving Killeen On An Eagle

(for Audell Shelburne)

Soldiers of the 1st Cavalry come & go
Wearing uniforms for a desert—
Sand-shades, dunes & stones;
Duffel bags come & go.

With soldiers & their wives
I rise on a night of the new moon
Veiled behind a skein of rain.
Off the port wing on the earth below

It seems constellations have fallen
As we fly higher. Burning coals
Spilled across the dark horizon mark
The end of the world; glitter trails glow.

I have flown over the world
On the eve of the Epiphany
Leaving a scene of three panels painted:
A triptych rendered sage brush, desert,

Red rocks—a landscape of mesa &
Mystery. I reflect on the vision;
A voice gives up a line before paintings.
Poets, story tellers & singers

Lived inside the art of the landscape
For a moment or two sharing gifts—
A word, an image before a mesa—
Offered as on an altar.

One voice came as a prophet
To tell of lunar-like White Sands; another
Spoke of apricots melting in his hands;
One played hide & seek on horseback.

I imagined seeing icons,
I heard chants—a litany of elegies;
I glimpsed a mountain holy in my mind,
Landed on earth to find the Magi's star fallen.

"Louise's Lemons" watercolor by Sharon Lang

LEMON LOUD

I sound, I resound, I scream
until I thrust myself into the core
—Van Gogh—of the retina, ripping it.

> —Rafael Alberti,
> *"Amarillo" (29)*

Kandinsky Rondeau

The blue rider moves like a melody
Across the canvas. Folk art or fable.
Scene full of tremors, a soul surrenders.
The white toy horse is an epiphany
For *The Blue Rider.*

The Russian painter studies Monet's *Haystacks;*
Story and writer are horse and rider,
Or the paint and the painter, a flicker
Of childhood shapes, a gondola—abstract,
Like *The Blue Rider,*

In motion, black, long—on an inkblot sea.
Squeezed saxophone notes dance; an icon suddenly
Improvises a Tunisian dream, a small red reality.
Visualize a yellow Munich postal box; a canary
Sings for *The Blue Rider.*

Degas At The Races

He studied the masters in Paris.
Before the New Orleans scene,
He painted a wild stallion, Bucephalus—

The steed Alexander tamed. Mississippi
Makes its muddy moves on a slow track;
Degas rides upriver, leaving Creole levees.

In St. Louis he meets cotton traders
Shipping bales from his family's business.
From New Orleans to the Ohio River

By boat; from catfish to crystal and blue grass—
Strengthening Kentucky race horses restless
In his mind's eyes to run for the roses.

Landscape is a state of the eyes.
He sketches a swift steel-gray filly.
The art of a smart colt's moves arise

From the lithe agility, like a dancer
Disciplined by ballet. Intrigued,
Degas paints pastels, bathers.

Unlike Monet, working in open air,
Degas' art must never look accidental;
His compositions are of continuity. Breeder

And trainer settle the nervous tension,
Prepare their entry in the field of thirteen;
There is a drizzle. The day is leaden.

Reflecting on Paris, a fallen
Jockey in the steeple chase,
A carriage ride with the Valpincon

Family; Degas at Churchhill Downs
Sketches the paddock, the parade to the gate.
He retires to a studio away from the downs

To paint from charcoal drawings, focusing
On individual elements, compulsive for detail.
He creates a vision of speed—eye-bulging

Run in pastels—is the River City
Winner beating Captain B. down the stretch.
Zoom, crop, photo-finish: Silver Charm, jockey

In red silks on the inside,
Winner in gold and green running
Off the canvas, Freehouse outside

Partially shown; place and wind in closeup blur
Like bathers in layers of blue. A canvas wears
The winning jockey's silks. Visualize dancer

But paint a gray colt draped in a rose
Blanket; her breath *would not blow*
Out a candle—loose, composed

As a pet on a leash. Impressionist
Of the *Beaux Artes* brushes in Belmont,
Imagines Pimlico landscape, the Preakness.

The Triple Crown begins with a race for roses,
Horseflesh and silks in Baltimore. At Belmont
A legend breaks; flux and myth: no Bucephalus.

Memory-Keeper Of Cayo Hueso

The open green shade is his studio:
Palm trees, sour orange, sapodilla, mango.
He draws visions on bags of brown paper,
Offers art on an altar—a Singer
1930 sewing machine—chisels
Cypress with broken glass; horse-tails
Of hemp rope flick off razor cut wood chips.
He paints history cut in wood: fort of bricks
From Civil War, kites, a beach, yellow tail
Fish, a sign saying "Grunts & Grits." Novel
Lines—the lector reads Hemingway aloud;
Bahamas workers and Cubans hear clouds
Of words read as cigars roll—illustrations
Drawn like monks illuminating margins.

Feast Day In Toledo

Toledo-ware, black and gold for sale; El Greco's
Paintings drew us to the cathedral
On the granite promontory above the Rio Tajo.
His elongated figures, like icons, bless the hall
Of the sacristy; Byzantine, gaunt, mystical
Faces in oils burn bright with breath of bellows:
Our Lord in wintry reds taunted by the rabble.
  El Greco fired Toledo's forge.

Twisting streets, precipitous ravines, shadows.
In this steep landscape, St. Peter weeps, ethereal.
Prayers in pigment, El Greco's works echo.
Below cathedral windows awash with light-fall,
Light from eastern heavens hit the tabernacle
Illuminating the golden altar-hold,
The core of Toledo—fortress unassailable.
  El Greco—Toledo's Alchemist.

In the Jewish quarter he painted *The Burial
Of Count Orgaz*, for church of Santo Tome.
The painted, in torment, witness a miracle:
The crowd is aimless, lost at the funeral;
St. Augustine holds the Count's head; martyred
St. Stephen, stoned at his feet, a beaten anvil.
  El Greco forged Toledo's soul.

The rosemary petals are strewn, fragrant
And sharp on the cobblestones; *damasquinado*
Shops forge blades where Reds laid siege to Royalists.
  El Greco formed Toledo on an anvil.

Rondeau: Girl With Cello

(after an oil painting by Milton Avery in the Columbia Museum of Art)

He painted sonorities, vibrations of colors.
Abstract expressionist, yes, but he never lost
His sense of the figurative, intimate family ties
Represented without embellishments, colors
Formed, figures often in silhouette. His daughter

Playing a cello. Decorative. No bow. Left arm
Around the body, touching strings, blank face.
Daughter, March, reading, reclining, with an orchid;
His wife, Sally, posing nude, with a yellow guitar.
Milton Avery's first sale was to a friend, a violinist.

He painted sonorities, vibrations of colors
Hinting of Matisse; familiar earth tones, modernized,
Interlocked in space, flat as two-dimensional Japanese
Woodblock prints. His canvas is a harmony, allusions—
A Wallace Stevens poem, pieces of a lyric in colors.

Wyeth Country, Overcast

The road to Chad's Ford snaked with turns.
The sky was threatening; the day cool.
I passed a barn of books and drove
With the Brandywine River in slow time.
Cattle posed for a still-life painting
Lyrical as guitar, flute, and cello.
Landmark in ruins: a stone country home.
Across the road was the artist's barn, his studio.

The painter's gray stone home slouched
Like rocks on Maine's coast, keeping its secrets,
Staying in touch with the past. At The Museum
I looked out to the Brandywine through a window;
A cow became a sculpture. Wyeth created her flesh
With tempura and a dry brush: his neighbor in secret
Modeled—a German—radiant in reddish blonde hair.
She turned away, gave me her back on canvas;
The secret nude stood on a rock ledge facing darkness.

Helga's pictures were all about light on a woman, shadows.
She aged as he painted her in braids; now in kindness
She is caregiver bathing him, remembering her own flesh.

Bonnard's Blue Bather

Picture Marthe bathing in blues
And impressionist's greens.
She was always bathing,
Bath water lapping her breasts,
Lounging, modeling for Bonnard.
His wife was floating pigments,
Water lilies in pools, toweling,
Giving us her back. Imagine
Another man's wife coming alive
In a voyeur's dream—saying
She is in tears in her bathtub
After reading Kenneth Rexroth's
Poems. Then she sponges
Off her arms and legs.
Soon she will melt,
Blending into bathwater,
A lotus flower afloat,
An oily rainbow in water.
Rexroth's admirers say
He wrote love poems
For loveless times.

Dental Appointment (2)

Reclining as the dental hygienist
Cleans, the Cyclops eye burns. You go blind, dream
Of the wrought iron cow made by the dentist—
Dangling fork-teats. Weaned on artistic regime,
He sculpts, molds, shapes more than teeth, drilling
Cavities while he converses on van Gogh;
Finishing a filling, he describes visiting
Vincent's National gallery show—
Thick oils, hayfields, crows, a skull's
Teeth biting a cigarette: Death plays no fool.
The dentist welds, bends metal for art, works
Objects his dead father owned, forms a skull.
He shows you his father's bust—a head of tools:
Hammer-brain, 8 mm camera-eyes hard at work.

Palm Sunday

(for John Haines)

A maker came to town.
He was welcomed and feted.
People carried prayers into streets
From church with blessed palm fronds.
Dogwood petals proceeded
Rock Creek Park's leaves.

That night the new moon
Walked early and alone.
Our visitor spoke
Of how he made his first
Sculpture in this city,
Of clay, long ago. His master
Told him it was damned
Archaic, abstract: two
Cowled female figures—
One hand touched the womb
Of the other. *The Visitation*,
The artist called it. One
More cast of poured concrete:
Mother and Child. He won
Third prize at the Corcoran.

He studied, but he molded
No more clay; he went away
To live alone, learned
To work with words,
To savor arctic silence.

He returns to the playground
        Near the Anacostia River,
The Navy yard where he lived
As a child before shipping out
From Coronado to war in the Pacific.
He visits the Catholic Cathedral
        Near Dupont Circle, not far
From the White House swept
        Up in legislative lingo.

        Are you a believer?
        Yes, I am a believer.

No campaigner, he departs
Again, critic in the Capital,
        A sculptor of syllables
Who shapes the word of mouth
        For the snowscape page

        Unlikely to be popular
As a sculptor or scribe
        In a city awhirl
        In cherry blossoms,
Perishable as prayers.

Anna Akhamatova & Amadeo Modigliani

Her husband left her in Paris—wearing
A long slit-skirt and a wide brimmed
Straw hat with an ostrich feather
He had brought her from Abyssinia.

With a painter she roamed the Latin Quarter;
She met him the year before. Letters
Were exchanged; he wished he
Could understand her Russian poems.

He raced with her through the Louvre,
Stopping in the midst of Egyptian sculpture.
Seeing her profile, he drew her as a queen
In ancient coiffeur, a dancer along the Nile.

They moved together under moonlight
On the old streets behind the Pantheon;
They sat under an enormous umbrella
On a bench in pouring rain reciting

The verses of Verlaine in the Luxembourg
Gardens. Once she came to his studio
To find him gone. Miffed, she tossed
A red rose bouquet through an open window.

He was amazed to find the flowers
Spilled across his bed in the locked
Room—so beautifully displayed.
At night he walked, restlessly.

She recognized his footsteps below
Her window on the cobbled streets.
She too was awake; her gray-green eyes,
Snow leopard eyes, prowled the night skies—

So Joseph Brodsky described his "keening muse"
Of St. Petersburg. Anna was able to divine
Her countrymen's suffering minds. Awakened
By the painter's heart, her affliction

Became art. It was the hour before dawn
In her dreams; the shadow of the future
Fell long before it arrived; it knocked
At her window, shuffled below street lamps.

Future broke into her dreams and frightened
Her with grotesque Parisian scenes,
Envisioned by Beaudelaire. The future
Stalked her from a nearby hiding place.

She took Modi's sketch of her
When she left—treasured as her holy
Icon and the small portrait of Tsar Nikolay—
Returning to her husband's family *dacha*.

The icon on the wall of her room:
Christ in Prison. She played circus,
Entertaining the local villagers, pretending
To be a trick rider. She could stretch

Her long legs behind her head, they said,
Like "snake woman." Someone wrote
She was like a tall bird feathered in fog
From the murky Baltic, a bird

Used to flying—now dragging her wounded
Wing along the ground. In Slepnyovo,
Gumilyov praised her poems. In Paris,
A Jewish painter from Italy wasted.

Triptych: Manassas Studio

Three panels, three canvases, three easels
In the studio; three painters prepare,
Three palettes, two mix oils, one watercolors.

Three painters face an empty snowscape.
The canvas is white as the Easter sheeting
The women found in the resurrected tomb.

Three women remember not to be afraid:
One sees lavender ice and blue crystals;
One charcoals skeletal winter birch trees.

One of the three will wash on the sunlight.
She favors reds, but yellows abound
In her Battle Street garden watered with colors.

One of the painters hears earth tones—a hymn:
Great Falls, rocks of ages in the Potomac River,
Stone house textures, autumn hues, a church steeple.

A third does portraits, thinking of Sergeant's Lady X
In her strapless, black gown. On another easel
Two herons reveal a biblical passage.

One painter faces a storm's devastation
On the Outer banks. *I must paint this scene.*
To paint this day in this place is to save

The gift of light piercing a lugubrious sky.
Hearts ache as the light leaves, cut clouds heal.
The hand works—dips like a white heron's beak—

Create. Sable brushes daub pigments.
Earthy stones sing psalms. Tawny beast blesses
Us; lioness eyes memories of wilderness.

Genesis blooms: presence occupies a canvas—
Expressive as a mime's moves; silence dances
In viridian green, mauve, and cadmium

Scarlet—holy oils—a trio fulfills the emptiness.
Ancient icon imaged on cotton cloth: one vision
On three olive wood panels—hinged—inscribed.

Georgia O'Keeffe Remembers Texas

Before the crosses of New Mexico,
Before the bones and Ghost Ranch,
Before the blue petunia in a vase,
I tried to evangelize for art in Amarillo.

1913 photo: a lone figure on the brown plains;
I walk in winds and a wonderful emptiness.
Aesthetics is all about space, I would say,
And I asked for books from friends.

The art school library had only one book.
A teacher, I arranged displays of Greek
Pottery, textiles, and Persian plates.
Draw a window—a portal in a wall.

I remember riding the railroad to Amarillo,
To vertical blue brush stalks parted
White space, pooling in deep blue at the edge;
The adobe wall, the patio, the door drawn

First in charcoal—starting over—before
A large red poppy covered the canvas.
Always there is elimination, a choice,
Separation of space with something

Beautiful. So I shaped small sculptures,
Abstract, musical, as Kandinsky taught.
I recall distant dust of cattle drives. Chinese
Words—*the butterfly is a flower with wings.*

Please read to me from the *Book of Tea;*
Remind me of sky blue at the end of the world,
Of a young teacher painting canyons, learning to love
Dark window in white walls, corn, calligraphy,

Commanche moons. Measels hurt my eyes.
Weak from influenza, a lover's photography
Found me, helped me see symmetry, form
In found things: a rock, a cottonwood tree.

Stone Carver

(for Frederick Hart, 1943-1999)

In the beginning was a stone quarry.
You lean into its open heart,
Learn how the earth's heart breaks,
How the planet's core is mined,
Trace Indiana limestone in Virginia,
Cast spiraling galaxy in clay.
Heroic human shapes swirl
Out of your Chesley studio-vortex.

Sculpture is partial, what is left:
Crucifixion-shape sears a space
Through "Crux Gloria"—opens to sky;
Purcellville's St. Francis Parish.
Mute, your immobile gargoyles
Guard Washington Cathedral.
As God's mallet, you chiseled
His glory, letting chips fall in rural
Hollow where they may.

Under-study of the rock cutters,
You labored for Old World masters
Carvers, wounding shapes to life,
Containing your sculptor-ego,
Aspiring higher in the scaffolding.

Lightning—like Michelangelo's
Bolt on Sistine Chapel ceiling,
The finger of God—sent
A charge into your brain.
Your left arm hung limp. Working
You wondered about Bethoven
Losing his hearing, Milton blind.

Before the stroke, your spirit sparked
Ice-like Lucite. Legacy: *Daughters of Odessa,*
Four dancers; *Three Soldiers* in bronze
Jungle boots on the shore of a sea of names . . .

Your struggle produced a new Creation:
Out of Nothing—Adam—eyes closed,
Tongue seeks speech—wordless Eve—

Emerging incomplete. Some things stay;
Some things fall away. Art is partial:
A hole, a rock quarry for the soul.

Blues Train

The eleven-thirty-two passes through.
Box cars couple with tank cars. Night riders,
Like the woeful freight train's whistle, fade;
Smoldering ruby caboose is swallowed by the blues.

The eleven-thirty-two is passing through,
Passes Atlantic Research, Atlas Iron Works. At Bristow
Station crossing . . . bloodshot eyes blink and blaze . . . .
Roiling Crescent blurs by Appalachia, bound for bayous.

Soon Norfolk Southern's old steam engine 611
Will hoot west into the Shenandoah Valley,
Will blow down the line through the Blue Ridge.
The eleven-thirty-two is passing though,

Bridging the Rappahannock's rapids,
Smoking south to Richmond. Manassas Depot,
As the eleven-thirty-two is passing through,
Slumps in shadows beside the tracks, silent—

As after Confederate raid on Union stores; moody
Rhythms of the Night Riders in Warrenton slide along
Steel strings, cover the bass, thick as ground fog.
Tracks suture the wounds at Bull Run.

As the eleven-thirty-two passes through,
A breathless harmonica moans muddy delta blue.

Ballad For Forsythia

The sun daubs yellow, makes April's flower.
The wind is lion-like at the tail of a kite.
Flashy floods spill the frogs and worms ashore.
The silver drizzle is licking awake the light.
The street, sleek as a seal, swims black and bright,
As the thickets explode and our senses cloud;
The stunning new growth is shocking to our sight:
      The forsythia shrub is lemon loud.

We breathe in the swampy scents of muddy season;
The ripening aromas we know
Are whiffs of a resurrection passing reason,
Wilting in instants, as blooms go.
Our focus flashes. We miss the golden
And greening shoots uncoil, the bold show
Of mustard erupting—a commotion:
      The forsythia shrub is lemon loud.

So soon do hearts deafen, we hardly feel
The thrilling brush of feather, buff of cloud.
Before we turn too blind to birth, be still!
      The forsythia shrub is lemony and loud.

Louise In A Lemon Dream

The sun is a lemon, hot as lava flow;
In my dream I am driftwood; steamy
Meeting; salty murmurs swim to Miami,
Lapse along the beach. A feast of yellow
Ribbons honor servicemen and women,
Now. Not then. It was our time in the swells
And storms. Soon we were seas apart; fire fell
From wings of war bringing separation:
Once lost and found in tides, I remember
Lemon lamplight in palms, you tasting of mango
Ripening as Caribbean shudders.
Skies foretold the hurricane's heavy blows.
The lifeguard drowns in your lagoon-green eyes;
The cove of you rescues. We two survive.

Painting Dick Tracy Into Heaven

(after the paintings by Philip Morsberger in the Morris Museum of Art)

His father flew to heaven in a hat.
Painters are seers, so we hear prayers
As gazers, following the floating hat.

He paints figures in a rush, outlined, flat.
Impatient muralist—monk—at work making prayers.
His father comes from heaven as a hat.

Benedictines wear cassocks black as bats;
Artist's apprehension is reason for prayer—
Light from dark; red airplane—an acrobat.

Christ's Ascension in Bonnard's blues—from flat
Canvas where colors are pushed, shaped into prayers.
The Holy Ghost wears Dick Tracy's hat.

A fish symbol from catacombs? Is that
A gold fish from Matisse? Paintings are prayers,
Van Gogh's echoes; goggles find habitat—

Light—returning to funny papers, that
Joyful boy from Baltimore, at prayer;
He sees Golgotha in El Greco; at
The foot of the Cross, a clown; blessed be the hat.

Books In Al Basrah

The window is blocked solid: books
Saved from the maw of war. Muslims
And Christians in modern battles burn
Gilgamesh; *Qur'an* in parchment dies.
Memories of the Tigris and Euphrates
Are lost. One librarian is a savior;
Aided by her neighbors, she packed
Off *The Arabian Nights*; a few words
At a time escaped. Some neighbors
Could not read what they were saving.

An artist known for painting rooftop
Scenes of Naples saw windows as eyes:
Dark symmetry, blind stares, deep caves,
A skull's empty eye sockets.
Mondrian painted many grids,
Carefully lined out his canvas,
Composed perfect boxes, delicate
Black outlining one yellow square:
Mondrian's *(#9)*—an open
Window letting light in, lemon

Bright on the morning mosque.
Astrology found sanctuary;
A caliph's chronicles are refugees.
Fertile Crescent's minarets sing.
Mesopotamians view copies
Of Sumerian cuneiform
Tablets, Elamite voices sealed,
Drawings of a zigguarat, gods—
Illuminations—a zodiac,
Herodutus' writings on the Nile—

Leather bound by Egyptians—
Timbuktu to Baghdad to Basrah,
Hemmed in by Iraqi history.
Hadiths lean on *Ghazels*; a *Sufi
Manual* wedged between *Saladin*
And *Hammurabi.* Medical books
In Arabic from Mali. Calligraphy
From Cordoba was freed. Spice
Trade records sit on window sill.
Feel the bitter, the fragrant, the bright.

"Catherine and Hugh"

THE LATE FORGETTER

Holy Week

The bells of St. Dominic call us
To noon Mass in the nation's capital.
Merciless, we confess, seek forgiveness,

Thirsty for His mercy in Lenten duty.
Palm Sunday at Appomattox Court House:
Lee surrenders: Lincoln shot on Good Friday.

Catholics and Protestants wrestle Belfast
For peace in a divided province.
Civil war, terrorists, parades in past?

In Birmingham a twister tore
Loose trees from lines of thunder storms.
Anxious survivors thirst as before.

Japanese lanterns float the Tidal Basin.
Lemon time bombs go off—forsythia.
Lilacs give up the scent of Mary Magdalene—

First to arrive to anoint Easter's corpse.
At the empty tomb, a stranger in white
Robes says—as the sun rises, lighting copse

And cave, casting out darkness—*fear not.*
Sevilla's Cathedral bells drown out the Moors;
Muslims near Mecca's Grand Mosque get hot—

They stampede in a ritual "stoning
The devil" on their hajj—pilgrimage—
Entering a tragic paradise screaming.

Guatemalan bones chime in catacombs.
Pol Pot is the ashes of the Khmer Rouge.
Angor Wat is a perfect ruins of stones.

Buddha frowns. Beflowered *pasos*—Cordoba
Tipsy as St. Bernardo's hooded Brotherhood
Bears the weight of heavy floats; Sevilla's

Balconies shower *saetas* down on streets.
The vocalists are archers giving wings
To holy arrows wounding the weak,

Penitents in procession. The singers
Honor the Virgin and Christ crucified.
Good Friday dies in Spanish for sinners.

We are loved, but too weary to pray
In agonizing gardens shedding nipple-pink
And white petals, stripped and flogged this day

By the latest storms blamed on *El Nino*.
New fire ignites the Paschal candle.
Easter liturgy blesses incendiary glow.

May last suppers be sacramental
Meals of mahi mahi grilled on pita bread,
Consecrated wine—not just symbols.

Our rituals feed a faith. Stories unfold.
The pastor washes the feet of the Knights
Of Columbus playing disciples' roles.

Green onion shoots shudder in the chilling
Lingering rain. Weeds puff seeds on wings.
Old cherry bears new litter: pink sucklings.

The Gurney Man propels himself face down—
His legless roll peddling pencils in Charlotte.
Three papyrus fragments of Greek are found.

Matthew's Gospel may be an eye-witness
Account. Science now a buttress for faith?
Stigmata of azaleas renews, bloodless.

In a Baltimore gallery Claude Monet
Is going blind, sees through green glasses;
Wisteria and willows mark his way.

Lily-and-dogwood linen drapes an empty
Cross as Handel's *Alleluia* chorus rises.
Trappist monks drink the cup of Gethsemane.

Ash Wednesday, Roanoke

Holding the high ground, a church: trains
Keep prayer on the right side of the tracks

A Passover bridge for travelers, crowds
At noon Mass on the hill. A priest burns
Last Easter's palms in an iron bowl,
Blessing penitential soot in Lenten purple.

West of Lee's final retreat—a museum, rails
In a yard of surrendered engines. A rusty fire
Escape climbs from an alley on the urban edge
Of renewal. Foreheads smoked with crosses.

Joint Replacement Surgery

(for Louise)

Sinners on the edge can never wait, yet I wait, so late
To pray. I could celebrate the lavender myrtles, white crepes;
Ivory magnolia buds and blooms; the sweet gardenia
Garden's perfume; sunshine on wisteria.
I procrastinate before broken bone, shattered knee-cap.
Like Robert Redford—leading paratroopers: *A Bridge Too Far*,
Paddling his rubber boat across the river—repeating *Hail Mary*,
Full of grace, Hail Mary, full of grace . . . it's my fate to break
At the gate. "Outrageous" Barbaro—Pimlico favorite—Derby Winner
Snaps an ankle, breaks bones—quick jockey—Prado—dismounts
Saves the colt, the leg, not too late—just in time to bear the weight.
Her leg is human; surgeon straightens it, implants new joint, staples
The skin with stainless steel. I pray for her to heal; never too late
For faith, nor to put 27 pins in steed & learn: living in pain is not a race.

Stations

Since brass, nor stone, nor earth, nor boundless sea,
But sad mortality o'ersways their power . . .

—Sonnet 65, William Shakespeare

The priest swings his twisted leg, whistling,
Swinging on crutches between hall and church.
Thinking maybe he had been in an accident,
We return at dusk to join parishioners
In their prayers, making our way
Around the Stations of the Cross, stopping
At each wooden Cross shadowing the edge
Of the parking lot in Phoenix. The priest,
We can see now, is leading the procession
With one crutch on his left side. His right
Leg and right hand are maimed—
Yet he controls an amplifier for his voice
On what a stewardess would call a "wheelie."
By turns an elderly woman and young boy shine
A flashlight on the text the priest reads,
As he leads us to each sorrowful stop, pushing
His voice box on wheels with crippled hand,

Lugging his lameness. The sky is bruised
Purple, starless; blinking airliners
Crisscross over us; the priest's strong voice
Leads us through Christ's falls, lovingly leads
Us up to our souls on Golgotha, a shadowed peak
On Sonora Desert's rim. A crowd of shapes:
Face disfigured in dim light, a friar, an eye patch,
Silhouetted palm trees, saguaros cacti.
In the parking lot shadows a disabled
Priest makes music of birth defects on the edge
Of a resort, asking, on our behalf, for faith.
He does not question pain, asks for the ability
To accept mystery. We break up grateful, drift
Away like sand—remembering a cactus growing
Out of a stone wall, in bloom, at Taliesin West.
We also imagine medieval imagery, Holy Week,
Penitential sweats. Our cups of heartache
Taste like a gift—an oasis within a holy land.

Walking Stick

Feast of the Epiphany,
Remembering a journey,
Gifts of Three Kings,
At Mass where a priest
Makes music pulling,
Clinking the censor's chain,
Sprinkles incense grains
On charcoal in gold,
Swings smoking prayers—
Clouds of incense spread.
Old man with white hair
And white beard—like a
Greek Orthodox Bishop—
Kneels and rises with
The help of a hand-carved
Walking stick. He takes
The offertory gifts
To the sanctuary.
The handle of his staff
Is painted gold—
Carved into a grotto
Holding a painting:
The Virgin of Guadeloupe.
The old man plods
As bells call out noon.
Unlike a hermit,
Or a scary prophet,
He smiles, congenial,
Nods greetings—A gift-giver,
Seemingly serene
In his faith.
Mysterious, joyous
As Mexican poinsettias,
Provoking my own
Uncertainties.
His staff sings
With each swing:
Ave Maria.

Requiem On The Frontier Of Day

The work of mourning . . .
Bugles dead achievement . . . . —Geoffrey Hill

The body is an earthenware lamp.
The lamp's flame has gone out.
The flesh turns again to clay
As dirt is tossed on the pine box.

To everything there is a season . . .
A time to die; a time to plant . . . .
She left a yard of mangoes & avocados;
She moved to crepe myrtles & magnolias.

Cries in the night, loss, lamentations,
Anger, grief, love & grief returns again in
Waves on Key Biscayne, tides, ritual, wind
Stirring white caps, Old Testament & New.

She was the woman of needles & thread,
Helpful seamstress to neighbors, laboring
For daughter, learning late in her winter
Years of ancient Chinese tiles, creating

Gift bags for mah jongg players, new friends,
To hold their racks for bamboo & dragon tiles
& winds. She was born American in the Canal Zone
Where two oceans met in locks as cargo ships

& liners rose & fell. She was a mother in San Juan,
Moved to Miami to raise her daughter, touching
Greeks, Cubans & Jews, loving changing lives.
Hear the Spanish prayers; hear the Hebrew.

She is remembered by the Book of Wisdom,
Verses said from the Old Testament & New.
Her daughter bade farewell at Karla's;
Farewell—with *cafecitos Cubanos*, sweet—

To Coral Way. No pallbearer, but Cuban waiters
In Black tuxedos. No *arroz con pollo*, but *tostones*
With gray rice & black beans: Christians & Moors.
She died just after dawn, peaceful in her sleep.

After sending farewell signals across the miles
Back to Miami. At Olga's bier—graveside—near an
Aerodrome, the sun rose in flames translucent
Pinks became *a bright host, a wafer's whiteness.*

The daughter returned to her home, her rooms,
After the burial, to see a cardinal in flames outside
Her window—spiritual wings—a visitation. There is
A time for war & a time for peace. Her pain is no more,

Nor swelling; grief is deeper than her surgical wounds.
Pain in her flesh is no more. Love sustains the mourners
As we hear her soul sing, ascending on feathered wings.
Daughter flies higher than clouds, over Miami, over

Intense traffic, Hispanic streets to where heaven seems
Just over the horizon where ocean blues meet polar ice
& white caps blend in blue-greens old & new.
We pray the words of the Old Testament & the New.

O the cardinal flies red & hummingbirds miss her.
O the flesh grows old, cold as stone,
& dirt is our earth under stardust.
Her flesh is our flesh settling into our earth.

A woman—unknown to her daughter—saw her
Obituary & phoned from Coral Gables. For years
She searched for Olga who once had helped her.
In Olga's honor a votive candle burns in St. Sophia's

Chanticleer In The Caribbean

La Senora Ojea
Remembers Chanticleer's
Morning songs
In Sabana, Puerto Rico.
She loved the crowing
As much as rhythmic
Slow rains on tin roofs,
And open shutters, delicious
Swings in the hammock
Under the thatch shelter
At her grandfather's,
A land of green breezes.
He took her on the ferry ride
From Catano shanty town
Over to San Juan for *queso*
Derritido at La Bombonera.

Now the Bacardi distillery
Lures tourists there
With citrus-flavored rums.
Always afraid of birds,
Even their feathers,
She never neared the rooster
Who sang for her,
Knew only the silent "vane"
Turning in the wind for her,
The invisible singer
Of her childhood.

Now, returning
To her island, Chanticleer
Is still there, screwing
Around in Guaynabo,
A singer, a contrary protector
Of the hen house of his past,
Parading his cock's comb.
He calls out to her before daylight,
And later—as she is leaving—
Chanticleer sings out
At the San Juan airport
Crowing from a pet carrier—
A traveler too

Carted off someplace to fight
Illegally—maybe Maryland or Miami—
Aspiring to resume vocalizing
If he does not die entertaining.

Easter Sonnet

Easter lilies blare from the altar. A white breeze
By sunrise stirs purple cloth on a Cross;
Cloth whitens like dogwood petals on trees.
Spring beauty is temporary, our loss
Is everywhere—as the red azalea
Loses its flowers; pinks fade into green,
Washed clean as sheeting renewed in streams.
The women sing the first alleluias.

A body is missing; a cave empty.
When somebody we know turns up missing
It is hard to understand the mystery,
Harder still to celebrate. Start singing.
The stranger looks familiar as a prophecy.
Returning is all about the leaving.

April Near Beverly Mill

When the rooster-red dawn crowed,
The redbud bled—Judas tree hung
With purple vestments along Bull Run.
Late frost failed to flake the lemon leaf
Bushes huddling by a bridge abutment
Near Beverly Mill. A spatter of dogwood—
Mother-of-Pearl—marks the split-pine fence
Over the brass buried in the battlefield park.

       Orchards open
Parasols of apple blossoms,
Parade in the Shenandoah Valley,
White as an unwound shroud.
The Tidal Basin resurrects
Its Japanese cherry trees
      Unfolding like origami.
The season of new lambs—
Meals measured in sacred rites;
Green tea ceremony, pourings—
Carefully reveals itself:
Pink, tender as new wounds
     So we may believe.

Lost On Harmony Way

Leaving Interstate 64 is good for the soul.
Follow the scenic route in Southern Indiana,
Missing the right turn, lost well below

Little Egypt, Cairo, Illinois, where oil wells
Bob like large black birds, pumping,
Dunking—the cornfields' endless drills.

Coal-black pumps—the crows—deliver
The earth's ooze, squeezing fossil fuel
From the fields bordering Wabash River,

Hoosier state line. Van Gogh's gold,
Fertile soil, wheat, & corn waist high,
Yellow cut pasture, mowed hay rolled.

New Harmony—utopia—in Raintree County,
Fountains shaped as Orpheus' lyre; musical
Waters lost in a "rope walk" maze—not easy

Finding the center of the Harmonists' 19th century
Labyrinth—like Chartres Cathedral—a maze
Of patterns, pathways leading to eternity,

The earth's center, dead-ends, turns. Stop.
Listen. Go back. Reflect in the center;
Let someone pass; make a mistake; opt

Out. Walk on to read Rilke's *Advice*
To a Young Poet. Trappist monk Thomas Merton's
Words on a roofless church, a meditation space—

Not a traditional building. Merton reminds us
Religion is not the past, not then—but now,
Here. The Prophet, Jeremiah, says to us:

We are like the clay
In the potter's hands.
New Harmony's ways,

Circling, lives orbit on a potter's wheel.
Meditations on the sculpture: *Angel*
Of Harmony. Art enables us to feel:

Harmony outside St. Louis Basilica
Before crossing the Mississippi;
Stay off I-64—Poseyville, Cynthiana,

St. Joe, Indiana, Mesker Park Road,
Evansville. At St. Joseph Cemetery,
Another sculpture, another angel in the road.

Up the hill, turn on St. John's Drive, scan
The Indiana limestone for family name;
Find your mother's relatives if you can.

Get lost at 3 in the afternoon
Scanning headstones on 3 June, seeking
Gravestones on a Sunday afternoon.

Lost. Remember the last view—
Holes open under tents, caskets
Made by monks. It was June, you

Recall, a burial four years ago.
A faucet near a large elm.
A November burial nine years ago.

Widows water cut flowers alone.
Lamey is the wrong name. No graves so
Labeled. No father, no mother, a wife's stone

Unfound, husband's too unfound. Despair
In a garden of headstones . . . leaving—
Then a glimpse—Catherine's name—aware

At the eye's corner—Hugh cut into stone. Lemme
Anchors them side-by-side. Harmony finally
Is two graves found in the garden, not Lamey.

Harmony is lying face down
Where your parents graves are found,
Relieved to find the sacred ground,

To pray for the repose of their souls.
Old Main Street home came down
For a parking lot, empty space in Ohio

River town. Absence leaves east on the interstate;
Another wrong turn, double back to Archabbey;
Distracting traffic, hard to concentrate.

On high ground, above German farmers,
The Seminary. Lost traveler hears the bells
Calling the Benedictines to vespers.

St. Meinrad's bells count the hours,
Call out at three quarters
Past the 4 o'clock hour.

The way to vespers is the way
Of work, prayer, daily repentance,
The way to hospitality in the Archabbey.

The black robes enter the holy place
At 5 in the afternoon,
Like black bulls to a sacrificial space—

Open ring. Acceptance. Chapel space
Fills with their slow procession;
Chanting fills the hour with grace:

Hymns, psalms, & alleluias. Absence.
Archabbey of Indiana limestone
Intones renewal: music, ritual, silence.

Prayer leads to the center of the circle—
Where peace finds the Harmonists
As the travelers travel the circle.

Some will see the graceful limestone
Worked as a way in & out. See
Limestone turn to granite headstones,

A right turn, a restful stop. We learn
To call the gift of discovering the right way
Grace. Others wander looking for a turn

Of luck, along Harmony Way. In dejection,
We the living lie down with the dead. We lived
Holding a dying dog down for an injection.

The dead die with open eyes, loving,
Beloved, labored breathing heart-stopped.
The living remember the missing,

Hugging warm fur, giving up the ghost.
Love is a longing for our own redemption.
A loving beast is lost. Our ghosts

Leave life on scenic routes, at interstate-speeds,
Changing lanes. One gets lost walking
In battlefields, wishing the darkest deeds

Undone. Earth is no utopia, yet we embrace the dirt.
Dust to dust we pray. Hi Meadow is an inferno.
Bobcat Gulch burns. Ashes scatter. Blessed be the soot.

Poor Butterfly

Their love song was *Poor Butterfly*.
Now he stands at a window
And stares at O*le Buttermilk Sky*—
With little flecks of butter-
Gold where the sun rises.
Maybe he remembers his favorite tunes,
The ones the Hoosier crooned:

Hoagy Carmichael—who played piano
Accompanying his vocals.
Hoagy played in a movie,
Too, a match stick in his mouth,
With Bogey and Bacall, in the forties:
Hemingway's *To Have and Have Not*,
Filmed in the French Antilles.

The old widower dreams
As the morning package
Of the sky slowly
Unwraps itself, and the embers
Of a moon from long ago
Cool, kindle a new glow,
Burn through the tissue
Of the clouds in *Ole Buttermilk Sky.*
Like Hoagy—he hums *Poor Butterfly.*

The River Remembers

(for my father)

Your took two big quick last breaths
Like a Japanese pearl diver breath-
Holder beneath the surface swimmer
Reaching underwater reef breathless

Diver down after shells in the shallows
Following the sea sounds swimming
A seer among shells without air
You need air to breathe to be

In real life you were no able swimmer
So you put us in lakes and in rivers
You put us in pools enabling swimmers
Your children now make their ways

In waters without you on river bend
Border Indiana and Kentucky share
Return to horseshoe bend your headstone
Our mooring our anchor holding

Your breath below and above prayers
Breathe to be believers feel underground
River ebbing tide returns to the sea
Near where you sink deep now near

Your wife swimmers together again
Hear a heart-shaped shell ear remembers
We remember where Ohio River bends
Swimmers at last the river remembers.

Uncle Hugh, Shepherd

He would dismount at night to kindle coals
To comfort his hurt on the cold desert floor.
Hugh shook with the hack of his cough—
Alone with his flock of constellations.

Perhaps he was coughing, lost his balance;
Perhaps he was thrown—horse spooked,
Bucked him into the dust amidst the bleats
And the bells of his sheep. His lungs freed

At last from consumption—a breather
Free of TB rose over Arizona into stardust,
Returned to the fold. Now herdsman rover
Keeps his clouds' fleece safe forever.

Hitching Posts

My memory is a stone
Bowl, a fountain, a watering
Hole for horses in a traffic circle.
Hitching posts—black ring—
Wrought iron horses heads, corralled,
Wait, near Willard Library.
I was born in a river
Town, a Northerner. Across
The Ohio, Kentucky
Was the South. My father stopped
At the stone fountain before
I was born. He let his horse
Drink & rest along the route;
He drove horse & milk wagon.
My father saw his father-
In-law dying to escape
The loss of his job—harnessing
Horses at the Brewery stables.
The end of horse-drawn wagons
Ended his life's work, ended
My grandfather. I never knew him.
My son's daughters ride
A carriage pulled by a horse
In a woods in a Southern
Town where I own no horses.
But horses are big business.
Here in the autumn of my years
Horses have Right of Way.
They drink at the stone fountain
In a border town: my mind.

The Late Forgetter

(for my mother)

One of the late forgetters sleeps:
Whispers of a withering season,
A president murdered, tears,
My engagement to be married, her death;
Rituals, litanies, funeral pall,
Prayers, psalm for the repose of her soul.
In earth, by the Ohio River of her birth,
One of the late forgetters sleeps.

One of the late forgetters sleeps.
The call comes just two weeks past
The Mass we say for All Souls feast.
Brother and sisters begin to ask:
In what dark hour will her kingdom come?
I awaken to the telephone's refrain;
I hear her whisper, hear her call my name.
Her smile endures stone requiems.
One of the late forgetters sleeps.

One of the late forgetters sleeps
Deep into the core of her faith.
She tried to recognize the voice,
The nurse with her daughter's face.
Years ago, her memory wandered off
Like a child following a sunset, lost
In the Keys she struggled not to forget.
Puzzled, she tried to keep alive the light.
One of the late forgetters sleeps.

Memorials

Pearl Harbor: a white-as-bones memorial.
Our Hercules follows fighters to Guam;
With bomber crews we drank to dead airmen.
White bridge marks *Arizona's* burial.

SAC's Arc Light strikes, the ground tremors:
Year of the Snake, earth like cratered moon.
Sent my father a Tiki from monsoons,
The Polynesian god or ancestor.

A carving from the island of Oahu,
A war-like image in wood, father's gift
Stayed at home for three decades; then a shift:
Mother moved to nursing home. They lose

Their home to pay for care . . . adrift.
The refugee-carving looks for a home.
My gift, the Tiki, returns to me, its
Eyes stare from a formation, stares in stone—

Another memorial: low, black tomb—
Obsidian wall, cooled lava heals rift:
A mirror where clouds scroll and faces drift.
Feel the names. Put your fingers in the wounds.

A Couple Breathing

She
Curls—after the climb
To desire
On the summit.

He
Lies entwined
In her arms;
His arm cradles her neck.

Her leg rests
On his hip;
His arm rests
Beneath her breasts.

Their ascent
To the peak
Of the high pitch
Of *the little death*

Leads to descent.
Her breath rises
& falls like Eden
In his ear

Until
Their synchronous
Breathing links
An earthy peace

To dreams.
Dozing heartbeats
Pulse flesh tones—
All of love they know.

With A Double Thread

Sewing a once with a double thread
A shroud as well as a shift.
> —Thomas Hood, "The Song of the Shirt"

Some women needle with a double thread,
    Weaving with words a tapestry of dawn from night.
        These seamstresses sew for the living and the dead.

Devoted Penelope would weave her daily dread
    Keeping suitors at bay when unraveling at night.
        She sewed both shroud and shirt with a double thread.

Lovers of warriors bind their wounds, endure the wretched
    Needles in their hearts; thorns crown their twilight.
        A seamstress sews to keep the living from the dead.

Spinners and weavers make our cloth and spread
    Their fabrics before the ones who see the light
        Through needles' eyes, sewing with a double thread.

We stitch our giant quilts into a shroud,
    We sew and link our patchwork into memorial site;
        Threads of disease lace the laving to the dead.

Word-weavers tie their lines; sail-makers turn sacred
    Sail-cloth into shrouds, burials at sea. Recite
        With the sailors' wives, who knot with a double thread:
Blessed are those who clothe the living and the dead.

ACKNOWLEDGMENTS

Aries: "Aviatrix"

BlueLine: "Wings"

*Catfish Stew: "*Dental Appointment *(2),"*

Christianity and Literature: "Talkman," "The River Remembers"

Edge City Review: "April Near Beverly Mill"

Innisfree Poetry Journal: ""Triptych: Manassas Studio," "Joint Replacement Surgery"

Kakalak (anthology): "Riding In Kazakhstan"

Mountain Time (anthology): "Gods On Thin Ice"

New Texas 1999: "Georgia O'Keeffe Remembers Texas"

Permafrost: "Palm Sunday"

Petigru Review: "Closing Wounds"

The Poet's Domain (anthology): "Long Key," "The Narc's Wife Blows Smoke," "Chanticleer In The Caribbean," "Blues Train," "Poor Butterfly," "The Late Forgetter," "The Gargoyle's Stare," "With a Double Thread," "Ballad For Forsythia," "Uncle Hugh, Shepherd"

Potomac Review: "Hitching Posts"

Praesidium: "Flight Time," "Memorials," "Stone Carver," "Praying Dick Tracy Into Heaven"

Ruah: "Walking Stick"

Southern Revival (Deep Magic For Hurricane Relief: "Ivory Bill's Rondeau")

Tennessee Quarterly: ""After a Reading In The Folger Shakespeare Library"

Upstart Crow (A Shakespeare Journal): "Brass Reflections"

Windhover: ""Vulture Of The Ganges," "Leaving Killeen On An Eagle," "Holy Week," "Easter Sonnet," "Ash Wednesday, Roanoke," "Feast Day in Toledo," "Chaplain In The Gulf War," "Lost Along Harmony Way," "Recovering Speech In Lent," "Stations"

Yemassee: "Degas At The Races," "Memory-Keeper Of Cayo Hueso"

"Poor Butterfly," and "Louise In A Lemon Dream" also appeared in *Visions, Revisions*, a chapbook published by Ink Drop Press in 1994 in Painter, VA.

"Kandinsky Rondeau" and "Bonnard's Blue Bather" first appeared in a Mellen Poetry Press *anthology (2005)* Lewiston, NY, edited by Patricia Schultz (Mrs.). Published here with permission.
"Rondeau: *Girl With Cello*," "Wyeth Country, Overcast," "Books In *Al Bashra*,""The River Remembers," "With A Double Thread," "Aviatrix," "Vulture Of The Ganges" also appeared in *BRASS*, a chapbook published by the Poetry Society of South Carolina in Charleston, SC—winner of the Kinloch Rivers competition in 2006.

Note: p. 38 "Crux Gloria" is a 33 foot steel sculpture by Tomas J. Fernandez

p. 6 "Long Key" *in the bull ring of the moon* is from Garcia Lorca

ABOUT THE AUTHOR

Michael Hugh Lythgoe is a native of Indiana. He was educated at St. Louis University, The University of Notre Dame, and Bennington College, where he earned the Master of Fine Arts (MFA) degree in Writing and Literature. He served as an intelligence officer in the United States Air Force with assignments to Vietnam, Turkey, Spain, Libya, the United Kingdom, and several tours with the Defense Intelligence Agency. He also directed a joint service intelligence staff in Key West. Mike taught at Syracuse University, worked at the Smithsonian Association, and as a college administrator; he also directed an educational and research foundation. He has traveled extensively in Latin American and the Caribbean. He is married to the former Louise Serrano Ojea of Puerto Rico and Miami. They have two grown sons, and three granddaughters. The Lythgoes live in Aiken, SC where Mike serves as past president of the Academy For Life Long Learning at the USCA campus. He has published two poetry chapbooks: *Visions, Revisions* (Painter, VA 1994) and *BRASS* which won the Kinloch Rivers chapbook competition by the Poetry Society of South Carolina in 2006. He has read his poetry on NPR and his reading of Yusef Komunyakaa's poem, "Facing It," aired on the Lehrer Newshour (PBS); it is included in the Favorite Poems anthology and on the DVD *(An Invitation to Poetry,* edited by Robert Pinsky). Lythgoe has been a featured poet in the Frisson series at the Columbia Art Museum in company with a guitarist, and at the Morris Museum of Art in Augusta, GA. He was a featured poet at the 2007 Piccolo-Spoleto Arts Festival in Charleston, SC in 2007. Michael Lythgoe has published poems, reviews, interviews and critical essays. His credits include: *A Gradual Twilight* (essay on the poems of John Haines), *Windhover, The Writer's Chronicle, Christianity & Literature, Rock & Sling, The Caribbean Writer, Praesidium, Yemassee, Aries, Potomac Review,*

Permafrost, South Dakota Review, Kakalak, Passager, Innesfree Poetry Journal, The River, Easy Street Magazine, Upstart Crow (A Shakespeare Journal), New Texas, Ruah, Edge City Review, Catfish Stew, and the *Petigru Review.*